THE STANDARD RESPONSE PROTOCOL K12

Operational Guidance for Schools, Districts, Departments and Agencies
The "I Love U Guys" Foundation
SRP K12 Version 2.0

LOCKOUT LOCKDOWN EVACUATE SHELTER

SRP K12 Version 2.0 - 2015

PEACE

It does not mean to be in a place where there is no noise, trouble, or hard work.

It means to be in the midst of those things and still be calm in your heart.

STANDARD RESPONSE PROTOCOL

CHANGE HISTORY VERSION 2.0

AUTHOR/CONTRIBUTOR	VERSION	REVISION DATE	REVISION COMMENTARY
Russ Deffner John-Michael Keyes	2.0	01/08/2015	Version update. See: The Standard Response Protocol - V2 An Overview of What's New in the Standard Response Protocol

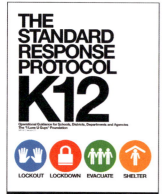

Operational Guidance for Schools, Districts, Departments and Agencies
A General Guide on Incorporating and Operating
The Standard Response Protocol within a School Safety Plan
Version 2.0
ISBN-13: 978-1507832738
ISBN-10: 1507832737

© Copyright 2009 - 2015, All rights reserved. The "I Love U Guys" Foundation. Bailey, CO 80421. SRP, The Standard Response Protocol and I Love U Guys are Trademarks of The "I Love U Guys" Foundation and may registered in certain jurisdictions.

THE "I LOVE U GUYS" FOUNDATION

On September 27th, 2006 a gunman entered Platte Canyon High School in Bailey, Colorado, held seven girls hostage and ultimately shot and killed Emily Keyes. During the time she was held hostage, Emily sent her parents text messages... "I love you guys" and "I love u guys. k?" Emily's kindness, spirit, fierce joy, and the dignity and grace that followed this tragic event define the core of The "I Love U Guys" Foundation.

MISSION

The "I Love U Guys" Foundation was created to restore and protect the joy of youth through educational programs and positive actions in collaboration with families, schools, communities, organizations and government entities.

TERMS OF USE

Schools, districts, departments, agencies and organizations may use these materials, at no cost, under the following conditions:

1. Materials are not re-sold.
2. Core actions and directives are not modified.
    2.1. Lockout - "Secure the Perimeter"
    2.2. Lockdown - "Locks, Lights, Out of Sight"
    2.3. Evacuate - *followed by a Location*
    2.4. Shelter - *followed by a hazard and safety strategy*
3. Notification of use is provided to The "I Love U Guys" Foundation through one of the following:
    3.1. Email notice to srp@iloveuguys.org
    3.2. Notice of Intent
    3.3. Memorandum of Understanding
4. The following modifications to the materials (Posters, handouts, cards) are allowable:
    4.1. Localization of evacuation events
    4.2. Localization of shelter events

CERTIFICATION PROGRAMS

The "I Love U Guys" Foundation is committed to providing its programs at no cost to a widening variety of organizations.

To assess the fidelity of implementation within an organization, the Foundation has developed a certification program for the Standard Response Protocol. The certification program is optional and is not required to use the SRP within your organization.

COPYRIGHTS AND TRADEMARKS

In order to protect the integrity and consistency of The Standard Response Protocol, The "I Love U Guys" Foundation exercises all protection under copyright and trademark. Use of this material is governed by the Terms of Use.

WARNINGS AND DISCLAIMER

Every effort has been made to make this book as complete and accurate as possible, but no warranty or fitness is implied. The information provided is on an "as is" basis.

AUTHOR/CONTRIBUTOR INFORMATION

John-Michael Keyes - Primary Author
The "I Love U Guys" Foundation
Executive Director
johnmichael@iloveuguys.org

Russell Deffner - Contributing Author
The "I Love U Guys" Foundation
Advisor/Contractor/Volunteer
russell@iloveuguys.org

Lee Shaughnessy - Reviewer
The "I Love U Guys" Foundation
Volunteer
lee@iloveuguys.org

Dr. David Benke - Teacher Guidance
The "I Love U Guys" Foundation
Board of Directors
david@iloveuguys.org

Janet Redford - Reviewer
The "I Love U Guys" Foundation
Volunteer

SPECIAL THANKS

Joleen Reefe - City and County of Broomfield (Joleen coined the phrase, "Locks, Lights, Out of Sight.")

Pat Hamilton - Executive Director of Operations, Adams 12 Five Star Schools

Kent Davies - Emergency Manager, City and County of Broomfield

John McDonald - Executive Director, Safety, Security and Emergency planning, Jefferson County Public Schools

Sergeant Heidi Walts - Broomfield Police

CONTACT INFORMATION

The "I Love U Guys" Foundation can be reached online at http://iloveuguys.org.

Email: srp@iloveuguys.org.

The "I Love U Guys" Foundation
PO Box 1230
Bailey, CO 80421
303.426.3100

EXECUTIVE DIRECTOR

John-Michael Keyes
johnmichael@iloveuguys.org

TABLE OF CONTENTS

Request for Comment	7
SRP Review Committee	7
Introduction	8
The Standard Response Protocol	9
SRP in a Nutshell	10
Protocol Details	11
Prerequisites	11
Lockout	12
Lockdown	13
Evacuate	14
Shelter	15
Hold	16
SRP V2	16
SRM V2	16
Lockdown Drill	17
Teacher Guidance	19
Frequently Asked Questions	21
Appendix A	23
Red/green/med/roll/alert cards	23
Appendix B	31
Posters and Handouts	31
Classroom Poster	31
Student Parent Handout Tell Parents How it Works	31
Classroom Response Poster	32
Public Address Protocol Poster	33
Appendix C	35
Notices and memorandums of understanding	35
Notice of Intent	36
MOU With The "I Love U Guys" Foundation	37
Sample MOU OR ADDENDUM With Law Enforcement/Fire/EMS	39

REQUEST FOR COMMENT

The Standard Response Protocol is a synthesis of common practices in use at a number of districts, departments and agencies. The evolution of SRP has included review, comment and suggestion from a number of practitioners. As of 2015, the SRP has been subjected to tactical scrutiny by hundreds of law enforcement agencies and operational review an adoption by thousands of schools.

Suggestions for modification can be made via email at srp_rfc@iloveuguys.org. Please include contact information, district, department or agency, including day time phone.

SRP REVIEW COMMITTEE

The "I Love U Guys" Foundation SRP Review Committee is comprised of safety stakeholders from a variety of perspectives and professions. The charter of the committee is to advise on the merits of any substantive changes to The Standard Response Protocol. This ensures that changes will not be incorporated into the SRP without consideration or deliberation.

The SRP Review Committee communicates on substantive changes to the SRP primarily through electronic means - Email or teleconference.

The following are the current members of the SRP Review Committee.

Dr. David Benke
The "I Love U Guys" Foundation
Bailey, Colorado

Sgt. AJ DeAndrea
Jefferson County Regional SWAT Team
Arvada, Colorado

Pat Hamilton
Director of Safe and Secure Environments
Adams 12 Five Star Schools
Thornton, Colorado

John-Michael Keyes
Executive Director, The "I Love U Guys" Foundation
Bailey, Colorado

John McDonald
Executive Director
Safety, Security and Emergency Planning
Jeffco Public Schools
Lakewood, Colorado

Louis J. Rapoli
Emergency Preparedness Consultant
Peregrine Training Services
Former NYPD
Newburgh, New York

Lee Shaughnessy
Vice President The "I Love U Guys" Foundation
Denver, Colorado

STANDARD™ RESPONSE PROTOCOL

INTRODUCTION

This document outlines The Standard Response Protocol (SRP) and offers guidance on incorporating this protocol into a school safety plan, for critical incident response within individual schools in a school district.

SRP IS NOT A REPLACEMENT... IT'S AN ENHANCEMENT TO YOUR EXISTING SAFETY PLANS.

The intent of this document is to provide basic guidance with respect for local conditions and authorities. The only mandate presented is that districts, agencies and departments retain the "Terms of Art" and "Directives" defined by this protocol.

SRP is not a replacement for any school safety plan or program. It is simply a classroom response enhancement for critical incidents, designed to provide consistent, clear, shared language and actions among all students, staff and first responders.

As a standard, SRP is being adopted by emergency managers, law enforcement, school and district administrators and emergency medical services across the country. Hundreds of agencies have evaluated the SRP and recommended the SRP to thousands of schools across the US and Canada.

New materials and updates can be found online at http://iloveuguys.org.

BEFORE YOU BEGIN

Districts and schools typically have a comprehensive safety program established and executed by dedicated safety or security personnel. That same, Safety Team, should be responsible for incorporating the SRP into the safety program. Having staff and including students on the Safety Team can greatly increase the buy-in and participation from all campus safety stakeholders.

If it was not done during the development of the existing safety program, it is highly encouraged that while incorporating the SRP, the safety team establish contact with local emergency services and law enforcement officials as they can help ensure safety plans will not conflict with existing local emergency services protocols.

A CRITICAL LOOK

Be prepared to look at existing plans with a critical eye as often they can be described as a "Directive" of a certain "Term of Art"; i.e. conducting a fire drill is practicing a specific type of evacuation and the actions performed are similar in all evacuation scenarios. It makes sense to teach and train broader evacuation techniques while testing or practicing a more specific directive, like evacuating to the parking lot due to a fire.

TIME BARRIERS

Time barriers or measures taken beforehand to 'harden the structure' can be an invaluable asset to safety; not only of staff and students, but also visitors to a campus who expect a friendly and secure environment.

Time Barriers are best described as a physical barrier that slows down the entry into or movement through a facility. Any additional delay allows trained persons to take further protective action and gives first responders more time to arrive.

A simple example of a Time Barrier would be making the exterior doors of a building automatically lock and could include installing a film on glass door panels to prevent them from shattering, delaying an intruder's attempt to break into the premises.

Finally, the most powerful time barrier in an active shooter event is a locked classroom door. Foundation investigation into past school shootings reveals that no person behind a locked classroom door has ever been physically harmed by an active shooter.

THE STANDARD RESPONSE PROTOCOL

A critical ingredient in the safe school recipe is the uniform classroom response to an incident at school. Weather events, fires, accidents, intruders and other threats to student safety are scenarios that are planned and trained for by school and district administration and staff.

Historically, schools have taken this scenario-based approach to respond to hazards and threats. It's not uncommon to find a stapled sheaf of papers or even a tabbed binder in a teacher's desk that describes a variety of things that might happen and the specific response to each event.

SRP IS ACTION BASED

The Standard Response Protocol is based not on individual scenarios but on the response to any given scenario. Like the Incident Command System (ICS), SRP demands a specific vocabulary but also allows for great flexibility. The premise is simple – there are four specific actions that can be performed during an incident. When communicating these actions, the action is labeled with a "Term of Art" and is then followed by a "Directive". Execution of the action is performed by active participants, including students, staff, teachers and first responders.

1. **Lockout** is followed by the Directive: "Secure the Perimeter" and is the protocol used to safeguard students and staff within the building.
2. **Lockdown** is followed by "Locks, Lights, Out of Sight" and is the protocol used to secure individual rooms and keep students quiet and in place.
3. **Evacuate** is always followed by a location, and is used to move students and staff from one location to a different location in or out of the building.
4. **Shelter** is always followed by the hazard and a safety strategy and is the protocol for group and self protection.

These specific actions can act as both a verb and a noun. If the action is Lockdown, it would be announced on public address as "Lockdown! Locks, Lights, Out of Sight." Communication to local Law Enforcement Agency would then be "We are under Lockdown."

Each response has specific student and staff action. The Evacuate response is always followed by a location: "Evacuate to the Bus Zone." Responses can also be chained. For instance, "Evacuate to Hallway. Shelter for Tornado. Drop, Cover and Hold."

BENEFITS

The benefits of SRP become quickly apparent. By standardizing the vocabulary, all stakeholders can understand the response and status of the event. For students, this provides continuity of expectations and actions throughout their educational career. For teachers, this becomes a simpler process to train and drill. For first responders, the common vocabulary and protocols establish a greater predictability that persists through the duration of an incident. Parents can easily understand the practices and can reinforce the protocol. Additionally, this protocol enables rapid response determination when an unforeseen event occurs.

The protocol also allows for a more predictable series of actions as an event unfolds. An intruder event may start as a Lockdown, but as the intruder is isolated, first responders would assist as parts of the school go to an "Evacuate to the Gym and Lockdown," and later "Evacuate to the Bus Zone."

LOCKOUT VS LOCKDOWN

The differentiation between Lockout and Lockdown is a critical element in SRP. A Lockout recovers all students from outside the building, secures the building perimeter and locks all outside doors. This would be implemented when there is a threat or hazard outside of the building. Criminal activity, dangerous events in the community, or even a vicious dog on the playground would be examples of a Lockout response. While the Lockout response encourages greater staff situational awareness, it allows for educational practices to continue with little classroom interruption or distraction.

Lockdown is a classroom-based protocol that requires locking the classroom door, turning off the lights and placing students out of sight of any corridor windows. Student action during Lockdown is to remain quiet. It does not mandate locking outside doors. There are several reasons for not locking perimeter doors during a Lockdown. Risk is increased to students or staff in exposed areas attempting to lock outside doors. Locking outside doors inhibits entry of first responders and increases risk as responders attempt to breach doors.

There may be situations where both Lockdown and Lockout need to be performed, but in this case they are identified individually. "Lockout! Secure the Perimeter. Lockdown! Locks, Lights, out of Sight." would be announced on public address. We are in "Lockdown and Lockout" would be conveyed to emergency services or 911.

TACTICAL RESPONSES

SRP also acknowledges that some school incidents involve a tactical response from law enforcement, and suggests consultation with local law enforcement regarding expectations and actions.

SRP IN A NUTSHELL
4 ACTIONS

Each protocol has specific staff and student actions that are unique to the action. In the event student or staff identifies the initial threat, calling 911 and administration is advised.

LOCKOUT - "SECURE THE PERIMETER"

Students are trained to:
- Return to inside of building
- Do business as usual

Teachers are trained to:
- Recover students and staff from outside building
- Increased situational awareness
- Take roll, account for students
- Do business as usual

LOCKDOWN - "LOCKS, LIGHTS, OUT OF SIGHT"

Students are trained to:
- Move away from sight
- Maintain silence

Teachers are trained to:
- Lock classroom door
- Lights out
- Move away from sight
- Maintain silence
- Do not open the door
- Take roll, account for students

EVACUATE - "TO A LOCATION"

Students are trained to:
- Leave stuff behind
- Bring their phone
- Form a single file line

Teachers are trained to:
- Grab roll sheet if possible
- Lead students to Evacuation location
- Take roll, account for students

SHELTER - "FOR HAZARD USING A SAFETY STRATEGY"

Hazards might include:
- Tornado
- Hazmat
- Earthquake
- Tsunami

Safety Strategies might include:
- Evacuate to shelter area
- Seal the room
- Drop, cover and hold
- Get to high ground

Students are trained in:
- Appropriate Hazards and Safety Strategies

Teachers are trained in:
- Appropriate Hazards and Safety Strategies
- Take roll, account for students
- Report injuries or problems, at the Evacuation Assembly, to first responders using Red Card/Green Card method.

1 DEMAND

The protocol also carries an obligation. Kids are smart. An implicit part of the SRP is that authorities and teachers tell them what's going on. Certainly, tempered at the elementary school. But middle school and above needs accurate information for the greatest survivability, to minimize panic and to mitigate recovery.

---

* Note: Student training includes preparation for some alternative methods during a tactical response but reinforces deference to local law enforcement.

PROTOCOL DETAILS
SUMMARY
This section of the guidance defines conditions, actions responsibilities and other aspects of preparing and incorporating The Standard Response Protocol within a school or district safety plan.

PREREQUISITES
NIMS CERTIFICATION
For full adherence to SRP the School and District Administration and Safety Teams must certify in the following Independent Study programs offered by the National Incident Management System (NIMS):

1. **IS 100** SCa Introduction to Incident Management for Schools
2. **IS 362** School Safety Planning

These courses are available online at http://training.fema.gov. Anticipate 1 to 3 hours per course to successfully achieve certification.

The courses are offered at no charge.

(Note: The "I Love U Guys" Foundation is not affiliated with FEMA.)

SCHOOL SAFETY PROGRAM
Schools incorporating SRP must have written safety plans and ongoing safety programs as identified in the the safety plan.

CREATING TIME BARRIERS
Historical data on active shooters suggests that a locked classroom door is a proven life saving strategy. Barricading is another option that has a positive track record. Self evacuation is another option. These strategies all provide a "Time Barrier" between students, assailants.

DOORS, LOCKS, STRESS AND FIRE MARSHALS
A consistent observation by first responders is that human beings, under stress, have difficulty completing even mundane tasks when they are under stress. The otherwise simple task of locking the classroom door may become extremely difficult for a teacher who has just heard a Lockdown order. Elevated adrenaline levels may result in the loss of fine motor skills and often result in extended times to insert a key and lock a door.

Keeping classroom doors locked during class, however, has proven to be disruptive, especially in high school classrooms. Propping a locked door might challenge some jurisdictions' fire code.

Adams County 12, Five Star Schools (Colorado) faced this challenge with a unique solution. Classroom doors in the district open out from the classroom. The keyed locks are in the doorknob, outside of the classroom. This means staff must stand in the hallway to actuate the lock, exposing them to risk during a Lockdown.

Adams County 12, Five Star Schools is using a simple, but effective workaround to solve this challenge. Flexible magnetic sheeting (such as refrigerator magnets) 1 3/4" x 6" are placed in the door jamb to prevent the door handle latch from catching. This allows the door to remain "locked" yet still allow access. In the event of a Lockdown, even highly stressed staff can readily pull the strip from inside of the jamb allowing the door lock.

TALK TO THE FIRE MARSHAL
It's important to talk to local fire authorities regarding this "Life Safety" solution. It may be relegated to only buildings with sprinkler systems. Code interpretation varies between authorities.

MEMORANDUMS OF UNDERSTANDING
Establishing Memorandums of Understanding (MOUs) between stakeholders is imperative. In many districts there is a handshake between the Superintendent and the Sheriff or Fire Marshal. Formalized MOUs are a requirement for full adherence to the SRP and should be reviewed and renewed on a scheduled basis.

LIAISONS AND OTHER MOUS
Schools and/or Districts should have a dedicated liaison and a Memorandum of Understanding with city, county or parish law enforcement agencies, fire departments, emergency medical services and emergency managers.

THE "I LOVE U GUYS" FOUNDATION MOUS OR NOTICE OF INTENT
Some schools, districts, departments and agencies may also desire a formalized MOU with The "I Love U Guys" Foundation. Sample MOUs are provided in this material for that purpose. The purpose of this MOU is to confirm adherence to the protocol by schools, districts, departments and agencies. It also confirms the online availability of the Foundation's materials.

An additional benefit for the Foundation is in seeking funding. Some private grantors view the MOU as a demonstration of program effectiveness.

Another option is to formally notify the foundation with a "Notice of Intent."

These are included within this material.

At a minimum, schools, districts, departments and agencies that will ultimately incorporate the SRP into their safety plans and practices should email srp@iloveuguys.org and let know.

LOCKOUT
CONDITION

Lockout is called when there is a threat or hazard **outside** of the school building. Whether it's due to violence or criminal activity in the immediate neighborhood, or a dangerous animal in the playground, Lockout uses the security of the physical facility to act as protection.

PUBLIC ADDRESS

The public address for Lockout is: **"Lockout! Secure the perimeter"** and is repeated twice each time the public address is performed.

ACTIONS

The Lockout Protocol demands bringing students into the main building and locking all outside access points.

Where possible, classroom activities would continue uninterrupted. Classes that were held outside, such as gym class, would return to the building and if possible continue class inside the building.

There may be occasions where students expect to be able to leave the building - end of classes, job commitment, etc. Depending on the condition, this may have to be prevented. During the training period, it should be emphasized to students as well as their parents that they may be inconvenienced by these directives, but their cooperation is important to ensure their safety.

INCIDENT COMMAND SYSTEM

The School Incident Command System should be initiated.

RESPONSIBILITY

Depending on the school, administration or teachers may be required to lock the doors or windows. Staff members assigned "Primary Responsibility" for a "Lockout Zone" should be identified in advance and should actively drill the protocol. These may include doorways, windows, loading docks, and fire escape ladder access points.

The assigned staff is designated as having **"Lockout Duty."**

There should also be assigned a person with "Secondary Responsibility" for Lockout Duty in the event the person with Primary Responsibility is absent or unable to perform the protocol.

Classroom teachers or instructors are required to take roll and determine if attendance has changed since the start of class. If there are extra or missing students, the teacher should notify the front office.

The front office should field information from the classrooms regarding missing or extra students in the classroom.

REPORTER

Lockout is typically reported by emergency dispatch to the school operator. The operator then informs administration and invokes the public address.

It may also be reported to the school operator by students, staff or teachers if a threat is directly observed outside of the building.

PREPARATION

Identification and of perimeter access points that must be locked in the event of a Lockout defines the **"Lockout Perimeter."**

Logical areas, building wings or other access point groupings define individual **"Lockout Zones"** within the Lockout Perimeter.

Some campuses may have campus perimeters in addition to building perimeters, such as gates and fences. There may be conditions where the campus perimeter would or would not be affected by Lockout.

Individual Lockout Duty Checklists should be created for each person assigned with either Primary or Secondary Lockout Duty.

Preparation includes identification of staff with Primary and Secondary responsibility and assignment of these duties.

DRILLS

Lockout drills should be performed twice a year. At least one of these drills should be performed while outdoor activities are in progress.

CONTINGENCIES

There may be physical attributes to the campus that mandate special handling of a Lockout. An example would be a campus where modular building are present. It may be best for students in modular buildings to Evacuate to the main building rather than going to Lockout in the modular building.

If during a Lockout a hazard manifests inside the school - i.e.: fire, flood, hazmat, then situational decisions must be made. It may be necessary to Evacuate to a different location than would typically be indicated, according to circumstances.

EXAMPLES OF LOCKOUT CONDITIONS

The following are some examples of when a school or emergency dispatch might call for a Lockout.

- Dangerous animal on school grounds
- Criminal activity in area
- Civil disobedience

LOCKDOWN
CONDITION

Lockdown is called when there is a threat or hazard **inside** the school building. From parental custody disputes to intruders to an active shooter, Lockdown uses classroom security to protect students and staff from threat.

PUBLIC ADDRESS

The public address for Lockdown is: **"Lockdown! Locks, Lights, Out of Sight!"** and is repeated twice each time the public address is performed.

ACTIONS

The Lockdown Protocol demands locking individual classroom doors or other access points, moving room occupants out of line of sight of the corridor windows and having room occupants maintain silence.

There is no call to action to lock the building outside access points. Rather, the protocol advises to leave the perimeter as is. The reasoning is simple - sending staff to lock outside doors exposes them to unnecessary risk and inhibits first responders entry into the building.

Teachers and student training reinforces the practice on **not** opening the classroom door, once in Lockdown. Rather, no indication of occupancy should be revealed until first responders open the door.

INCIDENT COMMAND SYSTEM

The School Incident Command System should be initiated.

RESPONSIBILITY

The classroom teacher is responsible for implementing Lockdown. The teacher should lock all classroom access points and facilitate moving occupants out of sight.

Silent or whispered roll should be taken to determine if attendance has changed since the beginning of class.

REPORTER

Lockdown is typically reported by students or staff to the school operator. The operator then invokes the public address and informs administration.

It may also be reported to the school operator by local emergency dispatch.

PREPARATION

Identification of classroom access points that must be locked in the event of a Lockdown is essential preparation. These may include doorways, windows, loading docks, and fire escape ladder access points.

A "safe zone" should also be identified within the classroom that is out of sight of the corridor window. Teachers and students should be trained to not open the classroom door until a first responder or school administration unlocks it.

Students, staff and teachers should be advised that a Lockdown may persist for several hours and during an incident, silence is essential.

DRILLS

Lockdown drills should be performed twice a year. If possible one of these drills should be performed with local law enforcement personnel participation. At a minimum, to comply with SRP, law enforcement participation in the drill should occur no less than once every 2 years. (For more information on drills see page

CONTINGENCIES

Students and staff who are outside of classrooms during a Lockdown may be faced with the need to get out of sight without the benefit of an empty or open classroom.

In this situation students and staff must be trained to hide or even Evacuate themselves away from the building.

If during a Lockdown an additional hazard manifests inside the school - i.e.: Fire, flood, hazmat, then situational decisions must be made. Evacuation to a non usual location may be required.

EXAMPLES OF LOCKDOWN CONDITIONS

The following are simply some examples of when a school or emergency dispatch might call for a Lockout.

- Dangerous animal within school building
- Intruder
- Angry or violent parent or student
- Active shooter

RED CARD/GREEN CARD

Some safety plans suggest sliding a red or green card under the door to indicate status. The SRP suggests this practice **not** be taken. Based on a number of tactical assessments, the overwhelming consensus is that this practice provides information to an armed intruder that there are potential targets in that room.

Please see the section on Red Card/Green Card/Med Card.

EVACUATE
CONDITION

Evacuate is called when there is a need to move students from one location to another.

PUBLIC ADDRESS

The public address for Evacuate is: **"Evacuate! To a Location"** and is repeated twice each time the public address is performed. For instance **"Evacuate! To the Flag Pole. Evacuate! To the Flag Pole."**

ACTIONS

The Evacuate Protocol demands students and staff move in an orderly fashion.

INCIDENT COMMAND SYSTEM

The School Incident Command System should be initiated.

RESPONSIBILITY

The classroom teacher is usually responsible for initiating an evacuation. In a police led evacuation, students may be instructed to form a single file line and hold hands front and back. Or students and staff may be asked to put their hands on their heads while evacuating. other directions may be invoked during an evacuation and student and staff should be prepared to follow specific instructions given by staff or first responders.

REPORTER

Evacuate is typically called by the school operator or in the case of a police led evacuation, by the responding officer.

PREPARATION

Evacuation preparation involves the identification of facility Evacuation Points, as well as student, teacher, and administrator training for both normal and police led evacuations

EVACUATION ASSEMBLY

The Evacuation Assembly refers to gathering at the Evacuation Assembly Point. Teachers are instructed to take roll after arrival at the Evacuation Assembly Point.

DRILLS

Evacuation drills should be performed twice a year. Fire drills constitute a valid evacuation drill. (Note: Fire Codes often mandate more frequent fire drills.)

INCIDENT COMMAND SYSTEM

The School Incident Command System should be initiated.

RED CARD/GREEN CARD/MED CARD

After taking roll the Red/Green/Med Card system is employed for administration or first responders to quickly, visually identify the status of the teachers' classes. (Select only one of the three card styles.)

- **Green Card (OK)** - All students accounted for, No immediate help is necessary
- **Red Card (Help)** - Extra or missing students, or vital information must be exchanged
- **Red and White Cross (Medical Help)** - Immediate medical attention is needed.

Schools may opt to use the SRP single sheet advisory which can be folded to any visual indicator.

RED CARD/GREEN CARD/ROLL CARD

An alternative design to the Red/Green/Med Card is the Red/Green/Roll Card.

RED CARD/GREEN CARD/ALERT CARD

Another alternative the Red/Green/Alert Card.

(Select only one of these three card styles.)

CONTINGENCIES

Students are trained that if they are separated from their class during an evacuation, then joining an evacuation line is acceptable. They should be instructed to identify themselves to the teacher in their group after arriving at the Evacuation site.

Special needs evacuation plans should be developed and drilled, including medication and pharmaceutical evacuation and chain of trust.

STANDARD REUNIFICATION METHOD

The "I Love U Guys" Foundation has developed guidance for reunifying parents with their children. These materials are available at no cost to districts, departments and agencies.

SHELTER
CONDITION

Shelter is called when the need for personal protection is necessary. Training should also include spontaneous events such as tornado, earthquake or hazmat.

PUBLIC ADDRESS

The public addresses for shelter should include the hazard and the safety strategy.

The public address is repeated twice each time the public address is performed.

HAZARDS MAY INCLUDE:
- Tornado
- Hazmat
- Earthquake
- Tsunami

SAFETY STRATEGIES MAY INCLUDE:
- Evacuate to shelter area
- Seal the room
- Drop, cover and hold
- Get to high ground

ACTIONS

Prior versions of the SRP sourced materials that were current on the FEMA website. As this FEMA guidance evolved, the FEMA information presented in SRP Operational Guidance became outdated.

It is strongly advised to remain current on both FEMA guidance regarding Shelter actions as well as local emergency manager guidance.

INCIDENT COMMAND SYSTEM

The School Incident Command System should be initiated.

RESPONSIBILITY

Each individual is responsible for sheltering. If there are special needs that prevent individual responsibility, administration should plan on how to best provide sheltering assistance.

REPORTER

Shelter is typically called by the school operator but may be called by students, teachers or first responders.

PREPARATION

Identification and marking of facility shelter areas.

DRILLS

Shelter safety strategies should be drilled once a year.

SHELTER - STATE THE HAZARD AND SAFETY STRATEGY VS. "SHELTER-IN-PLACE"

Oddly, one of the most often heard concerns about the SRP is the abandoning of "Shelter-in-place." The reason for this was simple. "Shelter-in-place" is contextual. Students and staff are somehow "supposed" to know which "Shelter-in-place" action to take.

During the initial development of the SRP, local, state and federal resources cited over a dozen different actions associated with "Shelter-in-place." Everything from hazmat to tornado to active violence to holding in a classroom were "Shelter-in-place" events.

PLAIN LANGUAGE ACT

With FEMA recommending plain, natural language,[1] the Foundation introduced the Shelter directive and suggested that rather than saying "In Place" as the action, identification of the hazard and the safety strategy would be more in keeping with the plain language commitment.

Shelter is one of the points where the SRP integrates tightly with school and district safety plans. Local hazards are very real and very important. If "Shelter-in-place" is part of emergency planner tradition and culture, it shouldn't be a stumbling block in implementing the SRP.

The goal of the SRP is that there is a shared, plain, natural language between students, staff and first responders. Evaluate how pervasive "Shelter-in-place" is, throughout the affected populations.

CUSTOMIZATION

The classroom poster is sufficient for generic Shelter guidance. The Foundation recognizes that localized hazards may need to be added to the poster. Original, digital artwork can be provided to organizations that have signed a "Notice of Intent" or a "Memorandum of Understanding" with The "I Love U Guys" Foundation.

Please note: Currently, original artwork is only provided in Mac OS X, Pages version 4.3 iWork '09. It may be compatible with Pages 6.x for Mac OS X, iOS, or iWork for iCloud beta. Currently, artwork is not available for Microsoft® Word. See FAQs.

---

1. Our promise to you: Writing you can understand - https://www.fema.gov/plain-language-act (URL still active January 2015)

HOLD
IN YOUR CLASSROOM

There may be situations that require students to remain in their classrooms. For example, an altercation in the hallway may demand keeping students out of the halls until it is resolved.

The focus of the SRP was in using common language and expectations in a crisis, between students, staff and first responders. While we looked at "Hold in your Classroom" as a fifth action we realized that the action was almost exclusively a day to day operational demand rather than an action shared with first responders. (Although a medical emergency might warrant the action.)

With the mandate of "Keep it Simple," the decision was made to **not** make "Hold in your classroom" an SRP action at this time. That said, we received requests to include the concept and integrate it into classroom training and materials. While there are numerous variations the following guidelines have been established.

PUBLIC ADDRESS

The public address for Hold is: **"Hold in your classroom"** and is repeated twice each time the public address is performed.

ACTIONS

Students and teachers are to remain in their classroom, even if there is a scheduled class change, until the all clear is announced.

SRP V2
EXPANDED AUDIENCE

The old adage "Build a better mouse trap and they'll beat a path to your door," is apparently true. In developing the original Standard Response Protocol, The "I Love U Guys" Foundation knew that it was an all-hazards, every-age, solution to sharing common language, common actions, and common expectations of behavior, between those impacted by a crisis and first responders. But our mission was youth.

Even though the materials were geared to a K-12 environment, business and institutions made them work. From Credit Unions to Courthouses to Community Colleges to Cathedrals, the SRP has been integrated into safety plans in business, institutions and organizations across the US and Canada.

As a result, the Foundation has worked with safety professionals to create materials for all audiences. Additionally, we've documented "What's New" in the Standard Response Protocol. All digital materials are available at no cost at http://iloveuguys.org. Printed materials may be purchased through Amazon or the Foundation's eStore.

SRM V2

The Standard Reunification Method has also been updated.

What's New in SRP V2

Pre-K to Second Grade

K12 Guidance

College Guidance

Business Guidance

Certification

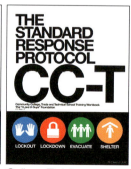
K12 Training

College Training

Business Training

Reunification

LOCKDOWN DRILL

INTRODUCTION

A critical aspect in implementing the SRP with fidelity is the Lockdown Drill. Successful drills provide participants with the "Muscle Memory" should an actual Lockdown occur. Drills also reveal deficiencies that may exist in either procedure or personnel.

PREPARATION

Prior to drilling, students, staff and administration should review the SRP Training Presentation (available at http://iloveuguys.org).

Administration should also verify with law enforcement their use of the SRP in the school or district.

Teachers should take time with students to identify and occupy a "Safe Zone" in the classroom where they cannot be seen through any corridor windows. If visibility in a classroom is problematic, alternative locations should be identified.

Additionally, the following instructions should be delivered to students.

1. Locate yourself at a point in the classroom where you can no longer see out the corridor window.
2. Maintain silence. No cell phone calls.
3. Refrain from texting during drills.

PARTNERSHIPS

School level drills should have district support. There may also be district resources available to assist in conducting the drill. Another key partnership is with local law enforcement. Local patrol, community resource officers or school resource officers should be part of the drill process.

THE EMERGENCY RESPONSE TEAM

A common practice is for the school to have a pre-identified Building/School Emergency Response Team. In a growing number of states, these teams are legislatively mandated to be organized using the Incident Command System. Even if not mandated, this structure is effective for responding to any type of incident and is used by other first responders.

It is not uncommon for administration to survey the staff population for prior emergency response, military or law enforcement experience for placement in the team.

THE LOCKDOWN DRILL TEAM

The Lockdown Drill Team is a little different than the Emergency Response Team. During an actual Lockdown, members of the Emergency Response Team may be in classrooms or administrative offices in Lockdown mode and unable to assist with the response.

The ideal Lockdown Drill Team should include the principal, facilities manager, district safety representatives and law enforcement. In larger schools it's important to have enough people on the team to conduct the drill in a timely manner.

STAFF NOTIFICATION

When Lockdown Drills are first being introduced to a school, it is absolutely okay to tell staff in advance of the drill. There may be staff members adversely affected by surprise drills.

SPECIAL NEEDS CONSIDERATIONS

It is critical to inform special needs staff prior to every drill. Some special needs students need advance notification that a drill is going to occur. For some students, any alteration to routine can be problematic.

THE PRE-DRILL BRIEFING

Prior to the Lockdown Drill a short planning meeting with the Lockdown Drill Team should occur. The agenda is simple:

1. Review the floor plan and team member assignments
2. Expected drill duration
3. The door knock and classroom conversation
4. Potential student or staff distress
5. Announcing the Lockdown Drill

When using public address to announce a Lockdown Drill, repeat, "Lockdown. Locks, Lights, Out of Sight. This is a drill." It's important to tell students and staff that this is a drill. Failure to do so will most likely result in parents, media and maybe even law enforcement coming to the school.

CONDUCTING THE DRILL

The Lockdown Drill Team should be broken into groups of two or three members who go to individual classrooms. One of the members acts as "Scribe" and documents each classroom response. (See Lockdown Response Worksheet.)

At the classroom door, team members listen for noise and look through the corridor window for any student or staff visibility or movement. A team member then knocks on the door and requests entry. There should be no response to this request.

At this point a member of the team unlocks the classroom door and announces their name and position.

THE CLASSROOM CONVERSATION

Typically this conversation addresses the purpose of the drill, and the observed outcome for that classroom. Additionally, self evacuation and other life safety strategies can be discussed. Any issues should be addressed gently but immediately.

WINDOWS

Often there is a conversation about inside and outside windows. Corridor windows are left uncovered so that first responders can see inside the room. Outside windows are left untouched because the threat would be inside the building.

THE LOCKDOWN DRILL TEAM DEBRIEF

At the conclusion of the drill, the team should reconvene for a debrief. Any issues should be documented and actions items should be identified.

LOCKDOWN DRILL
WORKSHEET

School _____

Date/Time _____

Team Members _____

_____

_____

Stopwatch Time _____ Student Population _____ Staff Count _____

Room#							
Locks	☐ Yes ☐ No	☐ Yes ☐ No	☐ Yes ☐ No	☐ Yes ☐ No	☐ Yes ☐ No	☐ Yes ☐ No	☐ Yes ☐ No
Lights	☐ Yes ☐ No	☐ Yes ☐ No	☐ Yes ☐ No	☐ Yes ☐ No	☐ Yes ☐ No	☐ Yes ☐ No	☐ Yes ☐ No
Out of Sight	☐ Yes ☐ No	☐ Yes ☐ No	☐ Yes ☐ No	☐ Yes ☐ No	☐ Yes ☐ No	☐ Yes ☐ No	☐ Yes ☐ No
Door Knock	☐ Yes ☐ No	☐ Yes ☐ No	☐ Yes ☐ No	☐ Yes ☐ No	☐ Yes ☐ No	☐ Yes ☐ No	☐ Yes ☐ No
Why?	☐ Yes ☐ No	☐ Yes ☐ No	☐ Yes ☐ No	☐ Yes ☐ No	☐ Yes ☐ No	☐ Yes ☐ No	☐ Yes ☐ No
Options	☐ Yes ☐ No	☐ Yes ☐ No	☐ Yes ☐ No	☐ Yes ☐ No	☐ Yes ☐ No	☐ Yes ☐ No	☐ Yes ☐ No

Notes _____

_____

_____

_____

Room#							
Locks	☐ Yes ☐ No	☐ Yes ☐ No	☐ Yes ☐ No	☐ Yes ☐ No	☐ Yes ☐ No	☐ Yes ☐ No	☐ Yes ☐ No
Lights	☐ Yes ☐ No	☐ Yes ☐ No	☐ Yes ☐ No	☐ Yes ☐ No	☐ Yes ☐ No	☐ Yes ☐ No	☐ Yes ☐ No
Out of Sight	☐ Yes ☐ No	☐ Yes ☐ No	☐ Yes ☐ No	☐ Yes ☐ No	☐ Yes ☐ No	☐ Yes ☐ No	☐ Yes ☐ No
Door Knock	☐ Yes ☐ No	☐ Yes ☐ No	☐ Yes ☐ No	☐ Yes ☐ No	☐ Yes ☐ No	☐ Yes ☐ No	☐ Yes ☐ No
Why?	☐ Yes ☐ No	☐ Yes ☐ No	☐ Yes ☐ No	☐ Yes ☐ No	☐ Yes ☐ No	☐ Yes ☐ No	☐ Yes ☐ No
Options	☐ Yes ☐ No	☐ Yes ☐ No	☐ Yes ☐ No	☐ Yes ☐ No	☐ Yes ☐ No	☐ Yes ☐ No	☐ Yes ☐ No

Notes _____

_____

_____

_____

TEACHER GUIDANCE
AFTER A LOCKDOWN DRILL

In 2010, Dr. David Benke tackled a gunman at Deer Creek Middle School in Littleton, Colorado. A 35 year veteran teacher, Dr. Benke offers his conversation with students after a Lockdown Drill. This is provided as guidance for for a conversation with students.

TALKING TO KIDS ABOUT THE SRP
There is a great deal of variation between elementary and high school. Elementary Students are much more willing to do what they are told. High school students always think they know better than adults. Perhaps with high school students our best goal is compliance rather than agreement.

BEFORE THE DRILL
This is important to insure that the drill is done well. Use the wall poster to get the conversation started.

Emphasize that the rules; no phones, silence, lights out, out of sight, locked doors, are all absolutes. Talking, poking each other, texting, will all result in a trip to administration and a requirement to redo the drill during lunch or after school until it is done perfectly.

THIS IS SERIOUS.
You are drilling to save lives. A phrase I found useful is, "I'm trying to keep you safe. I am not going to apologize for trying to save you.

Be sure the students know someone may come by to try the door. They are to maintain silence.

SAFE ZONE
Point out where the students are to sit and hide. Be sure to find an area that is not visible from a hall window. If a student can see out the hall window, a bad guy can see in.

Check the doors and windows to your room. Are they all lockable from the correct side? If they aren't, then submit an order to have the lock changed. I kept my door locked all the time. It took a year and three requests before we could get a lock changed. Be politely persistent.

DECIDE ON YOUR STATION IN THE ROOM.
Will you sit with the kids?

Will you station yourself in ambush with what ever improvised weapon you can find?

Play baseball during a free period with the kids once a year. It gives you an excuse to have a bat in your room.

AFTER THE DRILL
This is important for the students to do Scenario Based Thinking.

The first question is crucial. After the first one the students realize that it is really ok to ask and you will probably have to end the discussion after about 10 minutes when the "what ifs" start to become absurd.

Therefore you might want to prime the pump by asking. "How many of you wonder what would happen if you are... (in the hall, in the restroom, at lunch)?

Remember they aren't, just, trying to get out of class. I know your subject is important. You wouldn't want to teach it otherwise. But you are giving a kid a skill that is important for her entire life.

WHAT IF I AM IN THE HALL?
We will check the halls quickly before we lock and turn the lights out. Get to a classroom, any classroom, as quickly as you can and lock down.

If the classroom is already locked and lights out then find a place to hide. Do not go from classroom to classroom. We will not open the door for anyone because that person could be held hostage. If someone has a legitimate need to get in the room that person will have a key.

Call on students and ask if they have a thought about where to hide if they are in the hall. Talk about the difference between cover and concealment.

WHAT IF I AM AT LUNCH?
The same procedure applies.

WHAT IF I AM IN THE RESTROOM?
The same procedure applies.

WHAT IF A BAD GUY COMES IN THE ROOM?
The kids should know to evacuate. Tell them which door and to where, preferably to another room to lock down. Decide what you are going to do because the next question will be, "Mrs. Faversham? What are you going to do?"

WHAT IF I AM OUTSIDE?
Go to (name your evacuation site). Ask if they know how to get there. Discuss how
to get to the evacuation site the fastest way. Or get in the school, get in a classroom and lock
down.

Let the cops do their job. If you need help go to a teacher.

PUBLIC ADDRESS PROTOCOL

The public address is repeated twice each time the public address is performed.

The following represents the Public Address for The Standard Response Protocol

- **Lockout!** Secure the Perimeter
- **Lockdown!** Locks, Lights, out of Sight
- **Evacuate!** To a Location
- **Shelter!** For Hazard Using Safety Strategy

While SRP is an all hazard approach, the protocol suggests placement of scenario, public address posters near all reasonable public address systems.

CLASSROOM POSTERS

Part of a school's commitment to SRP is displaying posters in classrooms, libraries, cafeterias, gymnasiums auditoriums and hallways.

The Foundation recognizes that this commitment may impact printing budgets and consequently asks that schools or districts commit to a time frame when poster installation can be completed.

Downloadable templates are available for production of the posters at http://iloveuguys.org at no charge.

CELL PHONES

It is not uncommon for school administrators to ban cell phone use during a lockdown. Parent instincts may be at odds with that ban. Often, one of the first things a parent will do when there is a crisis in the school is text their child.

In evaluating actual lockdown events, the initial crisis may only take minutes. After the threat is mitigated, Law Enforcement typically clears the school one classroom at a time. This process may take significant time. During this time, both parents and students can reduce stress through text communications.

There is also an opportunity to ask the students to text their parents with crafted messages. For example, "Pick me up at Lincoln Elementary in one hour. Bring your ID."

TRAINING RESOURCES

The Foundation can provide on site training and has worked with a number of organizations in providing train the trainer sessions.

PROGRAM REVIEW

Reviewers of this material are available at http://iloveuguys.org

SRP REVIEW COMMITTEE

The SRP is locked at version 2. Substantive changes can now only made after committee review. Change requests can be emailed to srp_rfc@iloveuguys.org. Please include all contact information.

ADVANCED AND BASIC CERTIFICATION PROGRAMS

The "I Love U Guys" Foundation is committed to providing its programs at no cost to a widening variety of organizations.

To assess the fidelity of implementation within an organization, the Foundation has developed a certification program for the Standard Response Protocol. The certification program is optional and is not required to use the SRP within your organization. Two levels of certification are available - Basic Certification or Advanced Certification.

WHY CERTIFY?

Certification is another demonstration of your organization's commitment to safety. It shows that your organization meets baseline requirements in implementing the SRP.

WHAT'S IT COST?

The Basic Certification cost is $300 per organization and must be renewed every two years. The Advanced Certification cost is $1,000 in addition to training costs and demands on site training and evaluation by Foundation certified personnel.

Organizations are classified as follows:
- Public School District
- Community College Campus
- University Campus
- Private School Network
- Independent Private School
- Catholic Diocese
- Sheriff's Office
- Local Police
- Special Jurisdiction
- Tribal Police
- State Police/Highway Patrol
- Fire Protection District/Department
- Business Site
- Hospital Site

WHAT ARE THE REQUIREMENTS FOR CERTIFICATION?

For full details see our certification guides available online at iloveuguys.org, but in general include presence of an organization safety team, regular drills, training, public address protocols, partnerships between organizations and first responders and outreach to the organization's community.

Within those general guidelines are specific program objectives and procedures.

Advanced Certification includes all outcomes from the Basic Certification but also requires on-site training and evaluation.

ARE THERE ANY GRANTS AVAILABLE?

While we feel both certification programs are modestly priced, there is a grant process that can reduce or eliminate the certification costs.

STANDARD RESPONSE PROTOCOL

FREQUENTLY ASKED QUESTIONS

Since introducing the Standard Response Protocol in 2009, thousands of districts, departments and agencies have scrutinized, evaluated and ultimately implemented the program. During the process some questions seem to come up often.

SERIOUSLY, WHAT DOES IT REALLY COST?

Since its introduction in 2009, public K12 schools, districts, departments and agencies were free to use The "I Love U Guys" Foundation programs at no cost.

In 2015, the Foundation expanded availability, and now offers the programs to any public or private organization at no charge. Simply download the materials and begin the process.

WHAT ABOUT BUSINESS/CHURCH/INSTITUTION USE?

Please look at the materials designed specifically for institutional use on the website. http://iloveuguys.org.

I SEE YOU OFFER TRAINING, DO WE NEED TO BUY TRAINING IN ORDER TO USE THE PROGRAMS?

No. We've attempted to put enough material online so that schools and law enforcement can successfully implement Foundation programs. We know of thousands of schools across the US and Canada that have implemented the programs using internal resources.

That said, part of our sustainability model relies not just on charitable giving, but in providing training for districts departments and agencies. If your organization is interested in Foundation training, please contacts for rates and terms.

WHAT IS THE DIFFERENCE BETWEEN LOCKOUT AND LOCKDOWN AGAIN?

The term "Lockout" is used when there is a potential threat that can be mitigated by bringing everyone inside. It should be announced with the directive "Secure the Perimeter" which signals teachers and staff to lock exterior doors and while it calls for heightened situational awareness, allows for indoor activities to continue.

The term "Lockdown" means there is an active or imminent threat inside or nearby requiring immediate protective action. It is followed by the directive "Locks, Lights, Out of Sight" and requires locking classroom doors, turning out the lights, and remaining hidden until first responders arrive.

Effectively if the threat is outside the building, Lockout. If the threat is inside the building, Lockdown.

WHAT IF THE THREAT IS CLOSE TO THE BUILDING?

There may be situations where both a Lockout and a Lockdown may be called simultaneously. In this case securing the perimeter, securing the classroom and getting out of sight would be the practice.

IN LOCKDOWN, YOU SUGGEST UNLOCKING THE OUTSIDE DOORS. WHAT'S UP WITH THAT?

No. We don't. We occasionally hear this but our guidance is actually a little different. We suggest not putting anyone at risk by locking or unlocking outside doors. If the doors are locked leave them locked. Be sure you have a plan, in advance, that allows first responders the ability to enter the building quickly.

WON'T PEOPLE STILL COME IN THE BUILDING IF THE OUTSIDE DOORS ARE UNLOCKED DURING A LOCKDOWN?

Yes, people may be able to enter the building during the window of time between calling a Lockdown and the arrival of first responders.

A Lockdown is called when there is a life safety threat inside the building. During the development and throughout the lifecycle of the SRP, constant, deliberate scrutiny of all risk/benefit guidance is performed by the Foundation, district and law enforcement representatives. This has resulted in the Lockdown guidance provided.

That said, with any guidance provided, we defer to local decisions. If you are a district, please consult with your local law enforcement representatives for final guidance.

WHY ISN'T "HOLD IN YOUR CLASSROOM" AN SRP ACTION?

While we looked at "Hold in your Classroom" as a fifth action we realized that the action was almost exclusively a day to day operational demand rather than an action shared with first responders. We do include it in some classroom training materials as an optional addition.

I THOUGHT I SAW SHELTER GUIDANCE?

When we developed the SRP and released the first version in 2009 we included FEMA guidance regarding the Shelter directive and actions. FEMA changed that guidance in 2014. We are removing specific shelter guidance from our documentation and defer to the current practices published at http://fema.gov as well as your local emergency management guidance.

CAN THE SRP BE USED IN CONJUNCTION WITH OTHER SAFETY PLANS?

Yes, absolutely. The SRP is designed as an enhancement to any safety plan. It covers critical incidents by standardizing vocabulary so stakeholders can easily understand the status and respond quickly when an unforeseen event occurs. Comprehensive safety plans will include components such as communications, threat assessment, local hazards, operation continuity and reunification, amongst other items.

CAN I MODIFY MATERIALS?
That depends. The core actions and directives must remain intact. These are:

1. **Lockout** "Secure the Perimeter"
2. **Lockdown** "Locks, Lights, Out of Sight"
3. **Evacuate** followed by the announced location
4. **Shelter** followed by the announced hazard and safety strategy

Some details may need to be customized to your location. For instance, the classroom poster should be modified to include hazards and safety strategies that are specific to your location.

ARE THE SOURCE MATERIALS AVAILABLE?
Yes. Some of the materials are available. Original, digital artwork can be provided to organizations that have signed a "Notice of Intent" or a "Memorandum of Understanding" with The "I Love U Guys" Foundation.

Please note: Currently, original artwork is only provided in Mac OS X, Pages version 4.3 iWork '09.

CAN YOU SEND ME MATERIALS IN MICROSOFT WORD?
No. Retaining the graphic integrity of the materials proved beyond our capabilities using Microsoft Word.

CAN I REALLY USE THE MATERIALS? WHAT ABOUT COPYRIGHTS AND TRADEMARKS?
Schools, districts, departments, agencies and organizations are free to use the materials under the "Terms of Use" outlined in this document.

DO I NEED TO ASK PERMISSION TO USE THE MATERIALS?
No. You really don't need to ask permission. But, it would be fabulous if you let us know that you're using our programs.

DO I HAVE TO SIGN AN MOU WITH THE FOUNDATION?
It is not necessary to sign an MOU with the Foundation. But, please consider it. The Foundation is committed to providing programs at no cost. Yet, program development, enhancement and support are cost centers for us. One way we fund those costs is through private grants and funding.

An MOU is a strong demonstration of program validity and assists us with these types of funding requests.

DO I HAVE TO SEND A NOTICE OF INTENT?
In the absence of an MOU, a Notice of Intent provides similar value to us regarding demonstrations of program validity to potential funders.

DO I HAVE TO NOTIFY YOU AT ALL THAT I AM USING THE SRP?
We often speak with school safety stakeholders that have implemented the SRP, but hadn't quite mentioned it to us. Please, please, please let us know that your school, district, department or agency is using the SRP.

It is our goal that the SRP becomes the "Gold Standard." The more schools, districts, departments and agencies that we can show are using the program, the greater the chance for achieving our goal.

CAN I PUT OUR LOGO ON YOUR MATERIALS?
Yes. But with some caveats. If you are a school, district, department or agency you may include your logo on posters and handouts. If you are a commercial enterprise, please contact us in advance with intended usage.

In some states we have co-branding agreements with "umbrella" organizations. (Often school district self insurance pools.) In those states we ask that you also include the umbrella organizations branding.

Please see http://iloveuguys.org/cobranding for a list of current states and organizations.

WE WOULD LIKE TO PUT THE MATERIALS ON OUR WEBSITE.
Communication with your community is important. While you are free to place any material on your website, it's preferable that you link to the materials from our website. The reason for this is to allow us to track material usage. We can then use these numbers when we seek funding.

But, don't let that be a show stopper. If your IT group prefers, just copy the materials to your site.

DOES THE SRP WORK WITH "RUN, HIDE, FIGHT?"
In 2014, the Department of Education suggested "Run, Hide, Fight" as the preferred response to an active shooter. We don't believe the practice is mutually exclusive to the SRP. Again, consult with local law enforcement regarding your specific active shooter response.

There may be some challenges regarding training students using some of the "Run, Hide, Fight" materials available as of January 2015. The Department of Education suggests, *"These videos are not recommended for viewing by minors."*

(Citation - Circa 2015: http://rems.ed.gov/K12RespondToActiveShooter.aspx)

DOES THE SRP WORK WITH A.L.I.C.E.?
Again, we don't believe that SRP and A.L.I.C.E. are mutually exclusive.

DOES THE SRP WORK WITH "AVOID, DENY, DEFEND?"
The SRP attempts to be an all-hazards approach to school based events. Of all of the active shooter responses, our determination is that "Avoid, Deny, Defend" from Texas State University has the best positioning, linguistics and actions.

http://www.avoiddenydefend.org

APPENDIX A
RED/GREEN/MED/ROLL/ALERT CARDS

RED CARD / GREEN CARD / MED CARD / ROLL CARDS
Print-ready PDFs are available at http://iloveuguys.org

RED/GREEN/MED/ROLL CARD

Provided are three different versions of the SRP visual status indicator cards. One should be placed with a student roster in the classroom. During an Evacuation from the classroom, teachers should bring both the SRP card and the roster to Evacuation Assembly point. Teachers should fold the card to indicate status of the class or group.

While three different versions are available, please select the one that fits your practices. The following pages represent the fronts and backs of each version of the SRP card.

If you have missing or extra students or other non medical assistance needs, fold sheet to Help/Red.

Shown here is the Red/Green/Med Card. A quick introduction to the SRP is included on the front of the page.

During an Evacuation Assembly, the card can be folded for a quick, visual demonstration of status.

If you need immediate medical assistance, fold sheet to Medical Help.

Take roll, if no missing or extra students and everything else is OK, fold sheet to OK/Green. On the back of the sheet are other options.

Note: There may be tactical concerns about using the card system as a classroom status indicator. (Sliding the card under the door.)

SRP suggests consulting with local law enforcement about suggested practice.

Roll Sheet - Use this sheet to record names at an evacuation assembly point, also account for missing or extra staff and students

Missing Staff or Students

Extra Staff or Students

STANDARD RESPONSE PROTOCOL™

LOCKDOWN
LOCKS, LIGHTS, OUT OF SIGHT

Students are trained to:
- Move away from sight
- Maintain silence

Teachers are trained to:
- Lock classroom door
- Lights out
- Move away from sight
- Maintain silence
- Do not open the door
- Wait for first responders to open door
- Take roll, account for students

LOCKOUT
SECURE THE PERIMETER

Students are trained to:
- Return to inside of building
- Do business as usual

Teachers are trained to:
- Recover students and staff from outside building
- Increased situational awareness
- Take roll, account for students
- Do business as usual

EVACUATE
TO THE ANNOUNCED LOCATION

Students are trained to:
- Leave stuff behind
- Bring their phone

Teachers are trained to:
- Grab roll sheet if possible
- Lead students to evacuation location
- Take roll, account for students
- Report problems at the evacuation assembly using this card.

SHELTER
FOR A HAZARD USING SAFETY STRATEGY

Hazards might include:
- Tornado
- Hazmat

Safety Strategies might include:
- Evacuate to shelter area
- Seal the room

Students are trained in:
- Appropriate hazards and safety strategies

Teachers are trained in:
- Appropriate hazards and safety strategies
- Take roll, account for students

In the event of an evacuation, please take this card with you. To use this card during an Evacuation Assembly, fold along dotted lines so the appropriate message is outward facing.

© Copyright 2009-2015, All rights reserved. The "I Love U Guys" Foundation. Bailey, CO 80421. SRP, The Standard Response Protocol are Trademarks of The "I Love U Guys" Foundation. SRP K12 Version 2.0 - 2015

OK OK

HELP HELP

MEDICAL HELP

MEDICAL HELP

STANDARD RESPONSE PROTOCOL™

LOCKDOWN
LOCKS, LIGHTS, OUT OF SIGHT

Students are trained to:
- Move away from sight
- Maintain silence

Teachers are trained to:
- Lock classroom door
- Lights out
- Move away from sight
- Maintain silence
- Do not open the door
- Wait for first responders to open door
- Take roll, account for students

LOCKOUT
SECURE THE PERIMETER

Students are trained to:
- Return to inside of building
- Do business as usual

Teachers are trained to:
- Recover students and staff from outside building
- Increased situational awareness
- Take roll, account for students
- Do business as usual

EVACUATE
TO THE ANNOUNCED LOCATION

Students are trained to:
- Leave stuff behind
- Bring their phone

Teachers are trained to:
- Grab roll sheet if possible
- Lead students to evacuation location
- Take roll, account for students
- Report problems at the evacuation assembly using this card.

SHELTER
FOR A HAZARD USING SAFETY STRATEGY

Hazards might include:
- Tornado
- Hazmat

Safety Strategies might include:
- Evacuate to shelter area
- Seal the room

Students are trained in:
- Appropriate hazards and safety strategies

Teachers are trained in:
- Appropriate hazards and safety strategies
- Take roll, account for students

In the event of an evacuation, please take this card with you. To use this card during an Evacuation Assembly, fold along dotted lines so the appropriate message is outward facing.

© Copyright 2009-2015, All rights reserved. The "I Love U Guys" Foundation, Bailey, CO 80421. SRP, The Standard Response Protocol are Trademarks of The "I Love U Guys" Foundation. SRP K12 Version 2.0 - 2015

OK

OK

HELP

HELP

ALERT

ALERT

STANDARD RESPONSE PROTOCOL™

EVACUATE
TO THE ANNOUNCED LOCATION

Students are trained to:
- Leave stuff behind
- Bring their phone

Teachers are trained to:
- Grab roll sheet if possible
- Lead students to evacuation location
- Take roll, account for students
- Report problems at the evacuation assembly using this card.

LOCKDOWN
LOCKS, LIGHTS, OUT OF SIGHT

Students are trained to:
- Move away from sight
- Maintain silence

Teachers are trained to:
- Lock classroom door
- Lights out
- Move away from sight
- Maintain silence
- Do not open the door
- Wait for first responders to open door
- Take roll, account for students

LOCKOUT
SECURE THE PERIMETER

Students are trained to:
- Return to inside of building
- Do business as usual

Teachers are trained to:
- Recover students and staff from outside building
- Increased situational awareness
- Take roll, account for students
- Do business as usual

SHELTER
FOR A HAZARD USING SAFETY STRATEGY

Hazards might include:
- Tornado
- Hazmat

Safety Strategies might include:
- Evacuate to shelter area
- Seal the room

Students are trained in:
- Appropriate hazards and safety strategies

Teachers are trained in:
- Appropriate hazards and safety strategies
- Take roll, account for students

In the event of an evacuation, please take this card with you. *To use this card during an Evacuation Assembly, fold along dotted lines so the appropriate message is outward facing.*

© Copyright 2009-2015. All rights reserved. The "I Love U Guys" Foundation. Bailey, CO 80421. SRP, The Standard Response Protocol are Trademarks of The "I Love U Guys" Foundation. SRP K12 Version 2.0 - 2015

OK

OK

HELP

HELP

APPENDIX B
POSTERS AND HANDOUTS
CLASSROOM POSTER

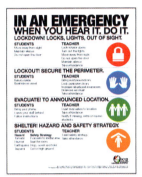

Placing Posters is an essential step in full implementation of the SRP. The classroom poster should be displayed in every classroom, near all entries, and near the entrances to cafeteria, auditorium and gym. The shelter hazards and safety strategies should be modified for local conditions.

PUBLIC ADDRESS POSTER

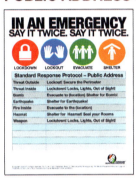

The Public Address Protocol Poster should be modified for the school's specific hazards and responses.

STUDENT PARENT HANDOUT
TELL PARENTS HOW IT WORKS

The Student Parent Handout is another useful tool in implementing the SRP. Many districts request that their schools send a copy home with students at the beginning of the school year and again prior to any planned drill.

It is also not uncommon to include the handout as an electronic attachment to email newsletters or safety related announcements.

IN AN EMERGENCY
WHEN YOU HEAR IT. DO IT.

LOCKDOWN! LOCKS, LIGHTS, OUT OF SIGHT.

STUDENTS
Move away from sight
Maintain silence
Do not open the door

TEACHER
Lock interior doors
Turn out the lights
Move away from sight
Do not open the door
Maintain silence
Take attendance

LOCKOUT! SECURE THE PERIMETER.

STUDENTS
Return inside
Business as usual

TEACHER
Bring everyone indoors
Lock perimeter doors
Increase situational awareness
Business as usual
Take attendance

EVACUATE! TO ANNOUNCED LOCATION.

STUDENTS
Bring your phone
Leave your stuff behind
Follow instructions

TEACHER
Lead evacuation to location
Take attendance
Notify if missing, extra or injured students

SHELTER! HAZARD AND SAFETY STRATEGY.

STUDENTS

Hazard	Safety Strategy
Tornado	Evacuate to shelter area
Hazmat	Seal the room
Earthquake	Drop, cover and hold
Tsunami	Get to high ground

TEACHER
Lead safety strategy
Take attendance

© Copyright 2009-2015, All Rights Reserved. The "I Love U Guys" Foundation. Bailey, CO. More info at http://iloveuguys.org.
The Standard Response Protocol and Logo are Trademarks of The "I Love U Guys" Foundation and may be registered in certain jurisdictions.

IN AN EMERGENCY
SAY IT TWICE. SAY IT TWICE.

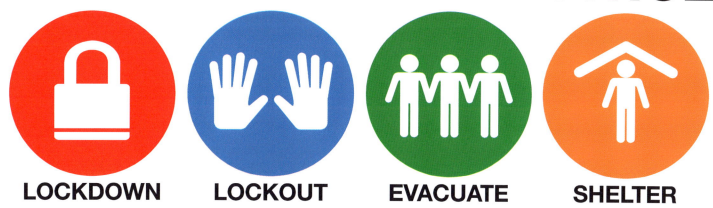

LOCKDOWN **LOCKOUT** **EVACUATE** **SHELTER**

Standard Response Protocol – Public Address	
Threat Outside	Lockout! Secure the Perimeter
Threat Inside	Lockdown! Locks, Lights, Out of Sight!
Bomb	Evacuate to (location) Shelter for Bomb!
Earthquake	Shelter for Earthquake!
Fire Inside	Evacuate to the (location)
Hazmat	Shelter for Hazmat! Seal your Rooms
Weapon	Lockdown! Locks, Lights, Out of Sight!

© Copyright 2009-2015, All Rights Reserved. The "I Love U Guys" Foundation. Bailey, CO. More info at http://iloveuguys.org. The Standard Response Protocol and Logo are Trademarks of The "I Love U Guys" Foundation and may be registered in certain jurisdictions.

STANDARD RESPONSE PROTOCOL

STUDENT SAFETY
A critical ingredient in the safe school recipe is the classroom response to an incident at school. Weather events, fire, accidents, intruders and other threats to student safety are scenarios that are planned and trained for by students, teachers, staff and administration.

SRP
Our school is expanding the safety program to include the Standard Response Protocol (SRP). The SRP is based on these four actions. Lockout, Lockdown, Evacuate and Shelter. In the event of an emergency, the action and appropriate direction will be called on the PA.

LOCKOUT - "Secure the Perimeter"
LOCKDOWN - "Locks, Lights, Out of Sight"
EVACUATE - "To the Announced Location"
SHELTER - "For a Hazard Using a Safety Strategy"

TRAINING
Please take a moment to review these actions. Students and staff will be trained and the school will drill these actions over the course of the school year.
More information can be found at
http://iloveuguys.org

LOCKOUT
SECURE THE PERIMETER
Lockout is called when there is a threat or hazard outside of the school building.

STUDENTS:
- Return to inside of building
- Do business as usual

TEACHERS
- Recover students and staff from outside building
- Increased situational awareness
- Do business as usual
- Take roll, account for students

LOCKDOWN
LOCKS, LIGHTS, OUT OF SIGHT
Lockdown is called when there is a threat or hazard inside the school building.

STUDENTS:
- Move away from sight
- Maintain silence

TEACHERS:
- Lock classroom door
- Lights out
- Move away from sight
- Maintain silence
- Wait for First Responders to open door
- Take roll, account for students

EVACUATE
TO A LOCATION
Evacuate is called to move students and staff from one location to another.

STUDENTS:
- Bring your phone
- Leave your stuff behind
- Form a single file line
- Show your hands
- Be prepared for alternatives during response.

TEACHERS:
- Grab roll sheet if possible
- Lead students to Evacuation Location
- Take roll, account for students

SHELTER
FOR A HAZARD USING SAFETY STRATEGY
Shelter is called when the need for personal protection is necessary.

SAMPLE HAZARDS:
- Tornado
- Hazmat

SAMPLE SAFETY STRATEGIES:
- Evacuate to shelter area
- Seal the room

STUDENTS:
- Appropriate hazards and safety strategies

TEACHERS:
- Appropriate hazards and safety strategies
- Take roll, account for students

© Copyright 2009-2014, All rights reserved. The "I Love U Guys" Foundation. Bailey, CO 80421. SRP, The Standard Response Protocol and I Love U Guys are Trademarks of The "I Love U Guys" Foundation and may registered in certain jurisdictions. This material may be duplicated for distribution by recognized schools, districts, departments and agencies.
SRP Handout for K12 | Version 2.0 | 01/08/2013 | Revised: 01/08/2013 | http://iloveuguys.org |

APPENDIX C
NOTICES AND MEMORANDUMS OF UNDERSTANDING

NOTICE OF INTENT
Name of School District (School District)
Standard Response Protocol (SRP)
Notice of Intent (MOU) to
The "I Love U Guys" Foundation (The Foundation)

PROGRAM DESCRIPTION
The Standard Response Protocol (SRP) is a classroom response based on four actions. When communicating these actions, the action is labeled with a "Term of Art" and is then followed by a Directive. Execution of the action is performed by active participants, including students, staff, teachers and first responders.

The "Term of Art" **Lockout** is followed by the Directive **"Secure the Perimeter"**. The action associated with Lockout is to bring participants into the School Building and secures the building's outside perimeter by locking appropriate windows, doors or other access points.

The "Term of Art" **Lockdown** is followed by the Directive **"Locks, Lights, Out of Sight"** The action associated with Lockdown is to secure individual classroom doors, move away from inside corridor line of sight and maintain silence until first responders release the room.

The "Term of Art" **Evacuate** is followed by the Directive **"To a Location"** (Where Location is announced.) The action associated with Evacuate is to move students and staff from one location to another.

The "Term of Art" **Shelter** is followed by the **"Hazard and Safety Strategy"** (Where Hazard may include: tornado, hazmat, bomb, tsunami, etc. Safety Strategy may include: seal the room, evacuate to shelter area, drop, cover and hold.) The action associated with Shelter is dependent on the stated Hazard and Safety Strategy.

COMMUNICATION
Communication between School District and The Foundation may be accomplished through written correspondence delivered by the US Postal Service or other private carriers. Communication may also be accomplished through electronic means utilizing electronic mail, facsimile or other electronic text communications.

PURPOSE
By standardizing vocabulary, all stakeholders can understand the response and status of the event. For students, this provides continuity of expectations and actions throughout their educational career. For teachers and staff this becomes a simpler process to train and drill. For first responders, the common vocabulary and protocols establish a greater predictability that persists through the duration of an incident. Parents can easily understand the practices and can reinforce the protocol. Additionally, this protocol enables rapid response determination when an unforeseen event occurs.

AGREEMENT BY SCHOOL DISTRICT
School District intends to incorporate SRP in the official, existing, written safety plans of all schools in district, either in the body or as an addendum or amendment.

MEMORANDUM TERM
This Memorandum is effective until terminated, for all schools in the School District.

TERMINATION
School District may terminate this Memorandum of Understanding via Written or Electronic notification at any time. Upon termination School District will cease use of any materials provided by The Foundation.

Name of School District
Address
City/State/Zip

_____   _____
Superintendent   Date

The "I Love U Guys" Foundation
PO Box 1230
Bailey, Colorado 80421

_____   _____
Executive Director   Date

MOU WITH THE "I LOVE U GUYS" FOUNDATION

Name of School District (School District)
Standard Response Protocol (SRP)
Memorandum of Understanding (MOU) with
The "I Love U Guys" Foundation (The Foundation)

PROGRAM DESCRIPTION

The Standard Response Protocol (SRP) is a classroom response based on four actions. When communicating these actions, the action is labeled with a "Term of Art" and is then followed by a Directive. Execution of the action is performed by active participants, including students, staff, teachers and first responders.

The "Term of Art" **Lockout** is followed by the Directive **"Secure the Perimeter"**. The action associated with Lockout is to bring participants into the School Building and secures the building's outside perimeter by locking appropriate windows, doors or other access points.

The "Term of Art" **Lockdown** is followed by the Directive **"Locks, Lights, Out of Sight"** The action associated with Lockdown is to secure individual classroom doors, move away from inside corridor line of sight and maintain silence until first responders release the room.

The "Term of Art" **Evacuate** is followed by the Directive **"To a Location"** (Where Location is announced.) The action associated with Evacuate is to move students and staff from one location to another.

The "Term of Art" **Shelter** is followed by the **"Hazard and Safety Strategy"** (Where Hazard may include: tornado, hazmat, bomb, tsunami, etc. Safety Strategy may include: seal the room, evacuate to shelter area, drop, cover and hold.) The action associated with Shelter is dependent on the stated Hazard and Safety Strategy.

COMMUNICATION

Communication between School District and The Foundation may be accomplished through written correspondence delivered by the US Postal Service or other private carriers. Communication may also be accomplished through electronic means utilizing electronic mail, facsimile or other electronic text communications.

PURPOSE

By standardizing vocabulary, all stakeholders can understand the response and status of the event. For students, this provides continuity of expectations and actions throughout their educational career. For teachers and staff this becomes a simpler process to train and drill. For first responders, the common vocabulary and protocols establish a greater predictability that persists through the duration of an incident. Parents can easily understand the practices and can reinforce the protocol. Additionally, this protocol enables rapid response determination when an unforeseen event occurs.

AGREEMENT BY SCHOOL DISTRICT

1. School District agrees to incorporate SRP in the official, existing, written safety plans of all schools in district, either in the body or as an addendum or amendment.
2. School District agrees to appoint an SRP Liaison who will act as the primary contact regarding communication with The Foundation and other department, district or agency SRP Liaisons.
3. School District agrees to incorporate the SRP using the terms of art and the associated directives as defined in the Program Description.
4. School District agrees to provide Law Enforcement Agencies having jurisdiction within the School District with notice of compliance with SRP terms of art and directives.
5. School District agrees to provide Fire Departments having jurisdiction within the School District with notice of compliance with SRP terms of art and directives.
6. School District agrees to provide Emergency Medical Services having jurisdiction within the School District with notice of compliance with SRP terms of art and directives.
7. School District agrees to provide County and/or City Emergency Managers having jurisdiction within the School District with notice of compliance with SRP terms of art and directives.
8. School District agrees to provide students with training on the SRP at least once per school year.
9. School District agrees to provide staff with training on the SRP at least once per school year.
10. School District agrees to drill each action.
11. School District agrees to provide parents with either printed material or notice of online availability of material at http://www.iloveuguys.org.
12. School District is responsible for physical material production of any online resources provided by The Foundation. The School District is not required to utilize printing services provided by The Foundation for production of support materials.

13. School District will provide The Foundation with 1 representative copy of printed or electronic materials produced from online materials provided by The Foundation.
14. School District will engage in a best effort to provide The Foundation with contact information for other agencies, departments, services, schools participating with the School District regarding the SRP.

AGREEMENT BY THE "I LOVE U GUYS" FOUNDATION
1. The Foundation agrees to host training materials on the Website available publicly at the Uniform Resource Locator http://iloveuguys.org
2. The Foundation agrees to provide implementation, support and training materials online at no additional charge for recognized organizations.
3. The Foundation agrees to provide implementation, support and training materials online to Law Enforcement Agencies at no charge to the Agency.
4. The Foundation agrees to provide implementation, support and training materials online to Fire Departments at no charge to the Department.
5. The Foundation agrees to provide implementation, support and training materials online to Emergency Medical Services at no charge to the Service.
6. The Foundation agrees to provide implementation, support and training materials online to County and/or City Emergency Managers at no charge to the County or City.
7. The Foundation provides training and certification opportunities online and in various locations around the United States at reasonable cost. School District is under no obligation to utilize training sessions or certification programs.
8. The Foundation will notify the SRP Liaison via Written or Electronic communications in the event of new or updated materials available on the Website.
9. The Foundation will maintain a record of all Written or Electronic communication with the School District.

MEMORANDUM TERM
This Memorandum is effective until terminated, for all schools in the School District.

TERMINATION
School District may terminate this Memorandum of Understanding via Written or Electronic notification at any time. Upon termination School District will cease use of any materials provided by The Foundation.

Name of School District
Address
City/State/Zip

_____   _____
Superintendent   Date

The "I Love U Guys" Foundation
PO Box 1230
Bailey, Colorado 80421

_____   _____
Executive Director   Date

SAMPLE MOU OR ADDENDUM WITH LAW ENFORCEMENT/FIRE/EMS

Name of School District (School District)
Standard Response Protocol (SRP)
Memorandum of Understanding (MOU) with
Name of Law/Fire/Medical Agency (Agency)

PROGRAM DESCRIPTION

The Standard Response Protocol (SRP) is a classroom response based on four actions. When communicating these actions, the action is labeled with a "Term of Art" and is then followed by a Directive. Execution of the action is performed by active participants, including Students, Staff, Teachers and First Responders.

The "Term of Art" **Lockout** is followed by the Directive **"Secure the Perimeter"**. The action associated with Lockout is to bring participants into the School Building and secures the building's outside perimeter by locking appropriate windows, doors or other access points.

The "Term of Art" **Lockdown** is followed by the Directive **"Locks, Lights, Out of Sight"** The action associated with Lockdown is to secure individual classroom doors, move away from inside corridor line of sight and maintain silence until first responders release the room.

The "Term of Art" **Evacuate** is followed by the Directive **"To a Location"** (Where Location is announced.) The action associated with Evacuate is to move students and staff from one location to another.

The "Term of Art" **Shelter** is followed by the **"Hazard and Safety Strategy"** (Where Hazard may include: tornado, hazmat, bomb, tsunami, etc. Safety Strategy may include: seal the room, evacuate to shelter area, drop, cover and hold.) The action associated with Shelter is dependent on the stated Hazard and Safety Strategy.

COMMUNICATION

Communication between School District and The Agency may be accomplished through written correspondence delivered by the US Postal Service or other private carriers. Communication may also be accomplished through electronic means utilizing electronic mail, facsimile or other electronic text communications.

PURPOSE

By standardizing vocabulary, all stakeholders can understand the response and status of the event. For students, this provides continuity of expectations and actions throughout their educational career. For teachers, this becomes a simpler process to train and drill. For first responders, the common vocabulary and protocols establish a greater predictability that persists through the duration of an incident. Parents can easily understand the practices and can reinforce the protocol. Additionally, this protocol enables rapid response determination when an unforeseen event occurs.

AGREEMENT BY SCHOOL DISTRICT

1. School District agrees to incorporate SRP in the official written safety plans of all schools in district, either in the body or as an addendum or amendment.
2. School District agrees to appoint an SRP Liaison who will act as the primary contact regarding communication with The Agency and other department, district or agency SRP Liaisons.
3. School District agrees to implement the SRP using the terms of art and the associated directives as defined in the Program Description.
4. School District agrees to provide Law Enforcement Agencies having jurisdiction within the School District with notice of compliance with SRP terms of art and directives.
5. School District agrees to provide Fire Departments having jurisdiction within the School District with notice of compliance with SRP terms of art and directives.
6. School District agrees to provide Emergency Medical Services having jurisdiction within the School District with notice of compliance with SRP terms of art and directives.
7. School District agrees to provide County and/or City Emergency Managers having jurisdiction within the School District with notice of compliance with SRP terms of art and directives.
8. School District agrees to provide students with training on the SRP at least once per school year.
9. School District agrees to provide staff with training on the SRP at least once per school year.
10. School District agrees to drill each action at a minimum of twice per school year per action.

AGREEMENT BY NAME OF LAW/FIRE/MEDICAL

1. The Agency agrees to incorporate SRP in the official written response plans of all schools in district, either in the body or as an addendum or amendment.

2. The Agency agrees to appoint an SRP Liaison who will act as the primary contact regarding communication with The Agency and other department, district or agency SRP Liaisons.
3. The Agency agrees to implement the SRP using the terms of art and the associated directives as defined in the Program Description.
4. The Agency agrees to provide Fire Departments having jurisdiction within the School District with notice of compliance with SRP terms of art and directives.
5. The Agency agrees to provide Emergency Medical Services having jurisdiction within the School District with notice of compliance with SRP terms of art and directives.
6. The Agency agrees to provide County and/or City Emergency Managers having jurisdiction within the School District with notice of compliance with SRP terms of art and directives.
7. The Agency agrees to train dispatch personnel in The Standard Response Protocol.
8. The Agency agrees to train School Resource Officers in The Standard Response Protocol.
9. The Agency agrees to train other appropriate personnel in The Standard Response Protocol.

MEMORANDUM TERM

This Memorandum is effective until terminated, for all schools in the School District.

TERMINATION

School District or Agency may terminate this Memorandum of Understanding via Written or Electronic notification at any time.

Name of School District
Address
City/State/Zip

_____   _____
Superintendent   Date

Name of Law/Fire/Medical
Address
City/State/Zip

_____   _____
Resource   Date

Made in the USA
Charleston, SC
10 July 2015